Companions of Life
Poems from Zimbabwe

Munyaradzi Mawere
&
Vakai Machinga

Langaa Research & Publishing CIG
Mankon, Bamenda

Publisher

Langaa RPCIG
Langaa Research & Publishing Common Initiative Group
P.O. Box 902 Mankon
Bamenda
North West Region
Cameroon
Langaagrp@gmail.com
www.langaa-rpcig.net

Distributed in and outside N. America by African Books Collective
orders@africanbookscollective.com
www.africanbookcollective.com

ISBN:9956-728-49-7

DISCLAIMER
All views expressed in this publication are those of the author and do
not necessarily reflect the views of Langaa RPCIG.

Table of Contents

Preface

This collection of erudite and finely crafted poems spans a wide range of topics and themes including love, weather, pieces of advice, environmentalism, morality, time, anxiety, politics, economics, justice and culture. The book expresses with great dexterity diverse issues: it is a product of vast life experiences across cultures and imaginative forays of the authors into socio-economic and political issues that haunt, boggle and dispirit humanity.

While the book powerfully questions an array of life phenomena, it aptly interrogates social evils that cut across all spheres of life such as bad governance, oppression, dissipation and injustice with some high degree of impartiality and cogency. Adopting the poetic license of liberal thinking and philosophical questioning, the authors encourage the spirit of critical thinking in all those who will have the privilege and honor to read a text such as the present.

The book, which is a collection of 93 thought out poems, is divided into two sections: Section A and B. The first section is a reflection of the authors' close examination, contact and passionate observation of critical questions and problems of people of diverse cultures within and beyond national boundaries. The section also offers possible solutions to numerous problems that threaten human existence. The second section of the book is a generous sharing of the authors' personal philosophies, life experiences and inner feelings.

For majority of students and instructors of English Literature and all those who cherish the merit of interdisciplinarity, especially from the disciplines of

Anthropology, Sociology and Cultural Studies, this is a collection they would enjoy reading. The collection seeks to show the wisdom and treasure of critical thinking. Above all else, the corpus of the book demonstrates the merit and power of poetry to question and question correctly all phenomena of life, and in upholding reticence.

Section A
Critical Reflections
And Questions on
Social Issues

Silent voices now speak

Hear now
Hear!
The whirlwinds of silent voices
That for centuries now
Had their lips sealed
Their tongues tied
Hear them now!
They speak

They are now weary
Of deafening noises of grenades
Of razing demolitions
Of merciless annihilations
Of ravaging desolations of nature
And ruthless mass destructions
Hear them now!
They speak

Hear what they speak of!
Total annihilation of the tyrant
Into the immeasurable depths of oblivion
Total restoration
Of their lost hopes
Total rejuvenation
Of their new hopes
Dazzling brilliance
Of their happy faces
And eternal serenity
Of their entire lives
Hear,
Silent voices now speak!

A glass of tears

How all desire to quench
From the Devil's dust land
To pluck light from darkness
To sing songs from the silent stone
To dare ignite frustration like a matchstick
To detonate the mind into insanity

How on wings of love to begin
To flap warily
To navigate through emotions
To command both speech and silence
To fight all tears with laughter
When drifts of dust
Terrorize forests with grave mounds
And weapons of mass destruction

How the impulses to dismiss
To arrest the world in handcuffs
To confront all probability and assumptions
With certainty and alacrity
To drive time to its electrocutions
And with reality so metaphoric
To capture all frustration in a glass of tears

So what exactly are you?

What exactly are you?
An animal?
A plant?
A condition?
So, what exactly are you?

Like morning dew
You evaporate in the sunrise
Like a chameleon
You transform your camouflage
Like seasons you change
But faster than lightning
Or even the rocket
Like a demon
You seize nations
Only to leave them ailing and crippled
Like bonfire smoke
You wiggle to unimagined heights
Where exactly to?
Nobody knows

So, shall we turn to n'angas
Or to medical doctors
To prophets
Or to God Himself
For interpretation

Who doesn't wobble where you set roots?
Remember in Zimbabwe
In the turn of the new millennium
Politicians, academicians, all citizens alike

Cried the same voice
Only because of you

You are studied everywhere
But it seems
No one fully comprehends you
Even Professors
And the most rationals of this land
Have failed you
So,
What exactly are you?

Cry no more

Pure your tears!
Gradual cascades of twilight,
Tears tender like dew drops
At the break of dawn
Gently,
Tears descend
To the cup of your dimples

Part the breeze's fur
The sun will surely rise!
And, new hope sprout!
Like fig tree shoots
In the season of spring

Cry not
Therefore,
Cry no more!

African Panorama

Here is the news:
The war is on the guns rattle
The people drown in the rain of grenade blasts
And choke in the smoke of illusory peace talks
The rebels cling to an eroded dream
Whose sand choke the dam we all drink from
The roads barricaded
Rockets wreck deep scars in children's faces
As they stare at the wet moon.
The banks close, all the money to the war effort
To defend the motherland of its dying people
We commend the government for such efforts
To extinguish a fire their arrogance had lit.

And…
The nights head in stitches
Crushes into the house like a painful headache.
This is the end of the bulletin,
Stay alert!

Blitzkrieg in the gutter of mind

Write from where the night roosts
And spreads its wings
Across the city
Marooned and demolished

Write as you pick the petals of despair
From the alleys you walk alone
Broke to the bone

Hungry to the look

Follow the night when it incubates
Misery, the desperate cries
The blitzkrieg of grenades in D.R.C

Write from the terror that storms the brain
The maniac at your groin
Human history such a loud fate!

Ebony my daughter

Where have your good morals gone?
I still remember those days
Those old days
When you were still a child
A child who knew how to kneel down
A child who knew how to greet people
A child who knew how to respect elders
A child who knew how to listen to parents
A child well born and bred

Ebony my daughter
Where then did you adopt this culture
A culture so baggy and corrupt
Is it from the metropolis
The so-called esteemed universities
The ghetto friends
Or the media?

Ebony my daughter
How you have become a rabid dog

A dog that spares nothing
A sword that cuts from all sides
A snake that bites from both ends
A spike that pierces from beneath
A flea that bites the bearer
A bow
So treacherous!
Ebony my daughter
Where have your good morals gone?

Walls sag

The walls sag
In our full gaze
The blaze of our hope
Whose intensity grow with its height
Burns out, dies in the rubble
The dust of it all
As it conquers the sky
Is the souvenir of our failed efforts
And when the tears fall
I know my love
We have lost all
We could never have gained

Money

Before you were here
There were no quarrels
No cries
Less crime
And treachery
You came
Like you wanted to help
But what a dangerous creature!
A flea that bites the host
A snake that chases the bearer
Shall we all run amok?

But who brought you
Here to this land
Peaceful land, Africa
Some say the Arabs
Others say the Whites
Whatever the case
You are a real case
A case that needs an answer

But let me know
This and only this small question:
Did you come for peace
Or to tear us into pieces
To make us wealthier
Or poorer than beggars
To make us smile
Or to cry to eternity
To withhold our peace
Or to quarrel till the second coming

Oh!
You seem adamant to answer
So,
Let me give a small advice
To all those who cherish
And enjoy your ride
That
They should put forth wisdom
And seek the glory of the Most High
Before they seek your comfort

Sketches of a nation on a blood sunset

I clinch the pebble of pain within
To smash your glassy conscience
The many dreams you have trodden to pulp
Branded with iron rods the sun till it grimaced!

And on the pages there is nothing
But a country with a sad history
A stubborn laughing stock
Sketched in blood strains
Sketches of a nation on a blood sunset

Who shall garner the courage
To tell you in frank words
That
An embrace begets adoration
As love begets love
And,
 A wrong cannot correct another wrong?

11

When shall you learn?
Dictators
Of a nation on a blood sunset!

Independence in prison

The history of this land
Paradoxical it is!

It all started
A so-called virgin land
A land
Peaceful and wealthy
A land
That everything lived on in harmony
As Adam and Eve did in Eden

What followed next?
Traders
Explorers and missionaries
Reign of terror from the South
And human mass carnage in the name of civilization

Then,
Came the so-called independence
But,
Tantalizing independence
Independence so illusory
Independence full of poverty
Independence full of contradictions
Independence with ravages of demolitions

Independence full of massacres
All in the name of freedom

What an independence?
Independence so paradoxical!

Going or Coming?

Like a wall watch
Time ticks away
Going!
But leaving traces

Though forward moving
Everything seems to follow
The principles of regression
And the logic of reduction
Like morning dew
Reduced to gas
Like soap
Reduced to foam
Like a mound of soil
Reduced to dust
Like a bundle of firewood
Reduced to ashes
Like the reasoning of an old man
Reduced to a toddler's thinking
So,
Are we coming or going?

While the hills are young

While the hills are young
And your skin shines in the sun
And your beauty sparkles in the night
And your laughter a tight twang
And your pace outpacing death
And your conviction a granite rock
And your caress an embrace of eternity
And your teeth blades of sunlight
And your tongue a flicker of lightning
And your breast a resolute will
And your eyes silent lullabies

While the hills are young
Make a bed of roses in the sunshine!

Everything Pays

Nothing doesn't pay
It pays to do bad
As it pays to do good
What only differs is the payment

Nothing doesn't pay
It pays to be lazy
As it pays to work hard
What only differs is the payment

Nothing doesn't pay
It pays to be unfaithful
As it pays to be faithful

What only differs is the payment

Nothing doesn't pay
It pays to hate
As it pays to love
What only differs is the payment

Nothing doesn't pay
It pays to be traitorous
As it pays to be honest
What only differs is the payment
So,
What doesn't pay?

Fruits of Thorns

Is this what I worked for,
What I toiled for
What I stockpiled
And safeguarded?

Is this what I gave birth to,
What I nursed
And nurtured?

Is this what I sowed,
What I watered
And nourished?

Is this what I planted,
What I weeded
And harvested?

Only fruits of thorns!

The last walk

In haste,
Peak ward, urgent
Towards the flaming hour
Of destiny
Struggling through entwined thistles
Voices
Anguished, agonized and bruised
Of our soul
Come!

Rusty streaks
Soon to go
Of sunlight
Tear through the eaves
This indeed is our last walk
Peak ward, urgent
To touch
The pea of purity

On the trail
As we curse through deception hedgerows
Are skulls scattered
Rattling and clattering
Of the thousands
Fallen
Desiring
And yearning
For freedom

This place used to be a thicket

Is this the place?
That place used to be a thicket
A place
Where rain used to fall all year round
A place
Where everything used to grow
A place
Where lions used to roar
A place
Where climbers used to trail around trees
A place
Where trees used to compete for sunlight
Is this the place?

Is this the place?
That place used to be the famous Hozvi thicket
A place
Where people used to help themselves behind trees
A place
Where people now use umbrellas to hide behind
A place
Where only tubers now grow
A place
Where baboons are now history
A place
Where rain now fall, but reach the ground not
Is this the place?

Elegy for a sad land

What words utter
The mind
An empty slate
Blank to depths
Silence the echoes in the gutter
A country silenced by its arrogance
Sheer rhetoric humdrum clichés
Action the gun barrel in the throat
Exhorting me to raise the open palm, the clinched fist
What speech with such reckless lies?
A million hopes pegged on those promises
Left to dry in the drilling sun

All questions answer the guns
More explanations from grenade blasts
The more defiant decay in Chikurubi

In children's eyes trails of uncertainty
A country collapsing
Our country, our hope
Sinking into the great depths of oblivion
Into insanity

Lundi River

At her will
Down the stretches of sand
Through imprisoning reeds
The river winds

Eager prints of sunrays on water
Translate my passion into song
We stroll,
You and me
Down the river bed
Where furled boughs bow,
Interlaced with innocence
We pass by the fish
In the pool
Which the vulgar flaming day,
Will not lure

With its imposing Staggering height above
The bridge lets no water through
But memories
And our saline lips tremble in an apocalypse
With each pebble you throw
The small tides shift
And the river runs her errands
Love toots a reed violin
The final voice of falling cascades
Echoes still in my heart
Come pose for a kiss
 Before we part

Alone on the road

Alone on the road
She travels
Stubborn
To the flaming catastrophe
Of darkness

She will not listen
Our jeering warnings
Or laughing murmurs

Alone in the marauding night
Trudging, stumbling and trembling
Defiant
To the Men-only sings on the road
To the mad dust of mockery
To the smitten fists of prejudice
Scything-
 Mowing down her sprouting hopes
Alone
Unarmed, up the glory trail
Knowing
There is no other time
No other moment except now
To reclaim what had been sucked
Out of her veins;
To gather her courage huddled
Under the moon
Wind-wiped in the darkness
Of all these wayward centuries

Perhaps not Knowing

Perhaps you may not know
What it means to be in a houseful of loneliness
Like expectant visitors

Not knowing
How the heart must burn in anguish
As the sun collapses beyond those mountains
Leaving behind a brooding darkness
With dying rays
To a brooding heart

Not knowing
How these walls must stare back
Amazed at how I must have stared at them
Pretending to see you

Why haven't you heard?

Why haven't you heard?
That half the population will be dead
A quarter more ailing
When floodgates open, prices run a stampede
That a thousand hopes will drop from school
Another million that will down their tools
A countless more dead, till the cemetery is full
That children no longer play violins
The zestless with no more from life to win
Except a country like waste paper in your bin!
Why haven't you heard?

Where shall you go?

The day is over
The merciless dark sun homeward descends
The ferocious dark that comes crushing on you
The thousand impatient stars that mock you
And the friendless night that loves you neither

Where then shall you go?
The past that glares with blood-shot eyes
The present like the mouth of a guillotine
The future a scrapyard
Of dreams dead
And nightmares
A journey
 That leads nowhere?

Sam

The seasons are dying
On those hill tops
And the balding heads of Gangare mountains
In the eyes of each horizon of hope
Comes scything the tearing vulture
Amputating with a blunt adze
Each from the rest

Sam, we always believe
We shall always meet
Always think we shall be together
To scratch and burst each other's pimples
And nurse, in mirth, time like a toddler

Sing to the wet moon
Those boyhood songs

No season meets its end willingly
Summer will cling to its last leaf
Winter like a bereaved orphan
Sobs to the window panes
Weeping but
But, weeping its debris for summer

Neither any man
Yet we seem to understand
How inevitable it is to die
Without our dreams winning the race
Nor our wishful thinking succumbs it all
For you have named your son
Tagarirofa.
We shall always die!

Predicament

This is time so difficult
Difficult to maneuver
To imagine
Or contemplate

This is time
Difficult to live in
Time
Where hunger gnaws
Head twinges
Body ails

And, death reeks

This is time
So difficult for freedom
Time
Where oppression is the subject of the day
Time
Where corruption is a cancer on land
Time
Where hardnosed dictators steal away freedom

This is time
Historic and unforgettable
Time
To reason and act

Armageddon

The end is surely at hand
The end, an all-conquering passion
Brother against brother,
Nation against nation
And the world against each other

Seas, in their silence swallow their pride
And the tall mountains crouch into the cradle
When He sets His feet to clean up his House

The drums throb
Trumpets burn their throats
Chariots for last hurry to the battle front
Where all must perish and vanish

In the flames of their blood
Neither Beast nor Whore of Babylon
Spared to see
Out of the barren desert
Seeds of hope sprout?

Full moon

We are here
Tired from the winding path
Across the arid deserts of humanity
Searching
Desperately
For the names of our souls
Lost in the harsh depth
Of a world
Dark
And frightening

Come!
Stretch your redeeming hand
Into the darkness
Where we stumble along
Searching
Frantically
For the grains of innocence
Lost to the passing wind

Pour us
Pour us back into ourselves
Back into the river of salvation
Where

At leisure
In the logic
Of ever changing ripples
We cruise in happiness

Give us
In these darkest hours of despair
Of civil wars, of decaying walls
Of corrupt officials

Give us ourselves
The reins to ride the chariots
Of our leaking conscience
So that never will we fall
Or stumble along the road

A wire of eternity

Memory's embrace
Bright as a mosaic
Of geranium flowers in a vase
Tightens me into its harbor
To sail on the tongue of wind
Recruiting in its strides
My lost life,
 Its debris,
Its shards
I look at the vast terrain
And the bold darkness coming in
Memory,
Tonight I shall
Embrace this stone of sleep

The name of eternity engraved on it.

Home coming

The Limpopo sings her song
Accompanying us our hearts pacing forth
To that hill
That red hill
We are singing revolutionary songs
Down the streets
Down the corridors
The harshly pronounced toll of the past
Is cast like a backdrop past our sight
And we see beyond the lacing of the sky
Please do not ask
Why we all these saline tears have
We are coming home with our broken hearts
We are singing funeral dirges
As the Limpopo runs deep at her will

A tether of barbed wire

Not knowing
How the disconsolate years have done
To me and a thousand more!
How the nights have passed on insistent feet
When abandoned memories from my heart
Hang on these bleak walls of exile!
How from the thick night the screams
Remind me of home and children
Threadbare, happy
Gathered on the recruiting warmth of the bonfire!

In me
These fragments
Shattered pieces of recollections
With memories they have struggled to preserve

Despite the savage torture
The soul had to endure
Persevere and persist
 Not knowing, my love
How the nights pass on insistent feet
Reminding me
How lonely
It must be on your part
To stare at the ceiling
Scratching desperately
The twang of memory
Those days we first met
And made our kiss
When the grass of home sung with us
The lonely emptiness here
Fills my mind
 With images of hope
That despite the chasm between us
I will free race and myself
To you
And rout the oppressor

Once again we will
Fall into each other's embrace,
My country

Mogadishu

The riffles
And sad memories of deafening AK
Announce such news bulletins,
Retelling the sad story at breakfast
With its ricochet in the red dust
Existence is all part of this wreckage
And clearly written is death's message

There is no hope
Neither tree nor shadow
To turn one's head in
Not even a morsel thin
Of tenderness to nurture the longing
In these children
Home is part of the nightmares
Bashing their tiny skies

And the future
Is thrown to them
In packets of rotting beans
And the future is limping
To the mass graves,
Decorated with wreaths
Of scars and wounds
And the future is decaying
With them there in the City of Death

Father to child

Look now my child!
The sun and how bright
From the deepest slumber of a timeless night
Clabbers up on trembling wings of a new day
And you are there
Embraced in the apocalypse
Of a new yearning life, the ray that shines

Hold your cry child
Oh my child
This is our land
Veined with worried streams of error to no end

Knit in the gossamer net of man's ways
And too, on these faces sometimes laughter flickers
But tears mostly do streak unpunctuated
It statements
Testimony to unending agony

Life,
Like a tide may rise,
 May fall
Yet to this life,
To this earth,
This is not all
Child,
Take now this, which I offer –my hand
Remember!
It was with a cry that you came
Perhaps to mourn the death,
Loaned you

Life?

And child
For only infractions this is home
We are bound to the land that gives and takes
The great cycles of birth and death
 That come and go
Of successes and of failures
Of wakefulness and slumber
And before death claims its pound of flesh
Remember child,
 When I am none,
When I am gone
Remember!
Life is a ride not to give up on

Rwanda 1999

Rwanda
Where the night goes
Mourners march slow
Pace after pace
And the giggling drum
And the lyre's broken anthem
And deaths ravaging rhythm
Pace with us up the red foothills

Madness' manacles manning our minds
Iron manacles in our hearts
In this mutilation, life is no art
Grief's thongs grip the heart

Seasons of sweet home memory
Burn in the shroud of shrapnel
Dust wafts into sorrowful song

Hunger stuck between a child's teeth
Between her sore breasts
A mother nurses the ghost of her child

There is nothing here
In every heart,
Only fear
In every heart
Only fear

Nothing Stays

We know less
For whom these words are meant
The nights come and go
With silent crying voices
Vast is the sky
That spreads before eyes
Hiding from us
The memories of those gone
We long to sing forever
In the pelt of rain
Yet nothing stays,
We all most yield to such vain.

Burning in the still rain

There is no such great pain
Like burning in the still rain
The mornings whose slumber on our doorsteps
Wakes us up to gape
 Amused at the red sunsets
We are there
 When we have not arrived
We heard clear
 The speeches of those who raved
Promising us
 More promises than the jobs
What more difference to make
When the difference to make is this chaos?
What more meaning to make
From these speeches?
And this waiting
Is the journey we are travelling
To that destination
Where more are kept waiting
For how long
Will we wait for them to keep us waiting
While in the still rain burning?
Burning!

Strange neighbors

A friend next door
She is almost invisible
Only her cooking a constant reminder
We hurl greetings through solid walls

Sometimes when in my drunken heavens
I suppose the smell of roasted meat or grass
Is smuggled by a resilient anxiety into my attic
Where no food roasts except this mind

One night she screamed,
Or was it me
The night shook,
its walls peeled off
After all she had it from her roasting
I, too
Like a madman burnt in my own!

Who shall hear our voices?

We stumble in the fog
And when we cry
Only empty nighty voices
Vibrate in the timbre of death
Our feet numb with fear
Grope hesitantly for answers
For a land greed has ravaged
Scotched in the veld fire

We stumble in the night

When the fog sets in
And when we cry
Only empty voices
Vibrate with the timbre of death

From a land laid bare
A land greed has ravaged
Scotched in the veld fire

We all seem to agree
That it is in today
That we have lost the future

When terror of the monster roars

Who on this earth would not worry
When terror's long tailed monster
Whose wings across the sky spreads
Roars in thunderous voice?

In a swoop
It shuttles across the yawning Atlantic
From the land of Dreamers, like a scavenger to besiege
In one gasp
It is Afghanistan bombed to a tinfoil
Across the Gulf vultures descend on the corpses of
peace
Those scattered skulls across the Arab's fields.

South African's ghost resurrects from the past
In one hand
A first of sea-weeds

In another
A tuft of bilingualism
While staggering from the hangover of racialism.

Zimbabwe
On its stone cobbled thoughts
Comes crumpling
Machete wielding conscience arching the monument
Into poignant torment
Red-eyed anarchy seizes the terrified moment
With bullets and baton -sticks
 In a staccato of raving speeches

Summer night

For they sing,
These children
Gathered around the wet moon
In the naked night

Though bare, their wet feet
Palter on these streets dancing,
Celebrating the emptiness
In us

But their sorrows
A flood
Remind me of the time of Noah

We
Perched high on the zenith
Watching the stretching of the rainbow

While high the flood rises

The end is near

The moment is of fear
The eye of terrible truth!
Action!
An impulse to tear
Never the loss to hear

No courage to face the end
Except to stumble on a guess
And even with much zest fight
The end that will take you
out of sight!

Still where I left you!

Still digging the same tired land
Still gagging a dry season
Still singing a chewed-out anthem
Still throwing slogans like grenades
Still pilling promises till hearts burst
Still nodding to the desperate platitudes
Still depending on borrowed confidence
Still the thumps-up sign for clear deception
Still fighting a war you have lost
Still killing to prove you are alive
Still plundering to replenish yesterday's plunder.

Prayer

In our limited wisdom we falter
We fall like dry meadow grass to the sword of the devil
We fall to the malady of hate
And with voracious appetite guzzle scorn

Lord!
 We are lost from your path
Straying into the dry sands of darkness
Where the jackals cavort and drool,
Striking down the lost, scattered desperate flock

Come now Lord!
Come!
Calm the roaring and rising seas, the scotching sun
Let our guns die, and wars sink beneath your feet
Let diseases perish into paralysis
Lord, cure us from this arrogance
Pour us out, and cast us unto the sea
Where we'll sure bathe in the glory of your
omnipresence
Once more huddled under the moon of innocence
We will reconcile with you, Our Maker!

A country called Zimbabwe

This is my country,
Zimbabwe
From whose people
Desperation's appetite consumes
All reasoning

So,
Shall you, the rational,
Resign to the pelting hailstorm,
Succumb to the delirious speeches
And lay to rest this gripping pain?

Shall you watch your voice of freedom
Swept away by the tide of time
While you huddle under the moon of fear?
Shall you once more sing
These gabbled songs of a glory long lost
And be the dying footsteps in the night?
Shall you yield to the baton sticks?
The ricochet of rabid rifles
And be counted as part of the statistics?

Remember!
For another five dry seasons of winter
You will once again draw
Clutching desperately
To this bunch of burnt-out straws?

Nightfall

Here is the full moon
Like a school late-comer
It peers
Over the shoulder of the mountain
Indeed
Night has come so soon
Its fingers grope
For the silent earth
Embracing its secrets with tenderness

Here
The hills stand like orphans
Abandoned and all alone
In the hearts of the moon-lit night
So it is with my heart
As the presence
Like ivy across abandoned walls.

Hope of Despair

Would you come
To speed me past
The long days of this, all the strife?

No more
Can I stand on my feet
Nor watch with my eyes
The face of defeat
So many
Have waded that flooded river

Where now I drown
 Into the vault of despair
So many more
Have climbed to the zenith
Yet my feet
Have become weary from the effort
So my days decay in the putrid heaps
Where many had theirs
Grown faster than cabbages
So I run
The entire mirage on the same spot

I am on that purposeful journey
That leads nowhere
All I see
Is this darkness brilliant
When so many follow
The rainbow to its end!
But never have the privilege
To comprehend its essence

Section B
Personal Philosophies
Life Experiences
Inner Feelings

You have fears too?

You too have fears
That the tongue may stick
To the roof of your mouth
Words that may run away
Mad and stray

You have fears
That before long
 Another war
So terrible like raw wounds
Salted and scratched
When the poor ignite ignorance
To blast might's monuments

You too have fears
That Zimbabwe is of stone
A country of monuments
Though monuments of cemeteries
A people gone with their precious ruined histories
That greed's veld fire
May maraud, pruning this plateau

A moon of nakedness

I
Bathe
In the moon
Of your nakedness
When
Desire
Burns
Like darkness between stars
Your body
A moon bathed landscape
I race
Up
Then
Down
Every peak
Till
I feel
Your reception
In that deep warm valley
Baffled and stunned
I sing
And
Sink
In delectation,
My wife!

A crazy world

This is a world
A world so ridiculous
A world where everyone is crazy
With some moment in day
To let loose the mind
To think of silly things
To think like toddlers
To imagine of the unimaginable
To worry of the unknown
Therefore,
The whole world is crazy

Anna

This is the honor
I am giving to you
The scent of roses
No one has received
The love
No one has enjoyed

In that small path
To the well nearby your homestead
We met
Baffled and stunned
With your charming beauty
My heart ran amok
My intestines
Rambling

How to start
This several miles away journey?
Only your commodious smile
That inviting smile
Filled me with alacrity
And, bolstered my courage

Bogus!
Was it the smile?
For indeed
You were a hard nut to crack

Only until then
That moment
You accepted my call
I knew that:
Everything is a journey
Even the love that we share
Also, a journey it is!

Grandpa

Old you are
But full of wisdom
Of charming character
And good deeds

Grandpa
Old you are
But full of love
Of fascinating tales
And words of advice

Grandpa
Old you are
But full of respect
Of valor
And self esteem

Grandpa
Old you are
But,
A role model to us all

A dry season

Sing to me
As the sun falls behind the hills
I knew tonight
Those cold hands I fear
Will the walls of my heart conquer?
Come let loose a river
Flood my heart with longing
And the dry grass
Sing the songs to the wide plains
I remember them too well now
Where I used to hide
Away from the wild beatings of home
My tongue is too heavy now
To sing once more as I used to
A love song plaited
With ribbons of the rainbow
As each day passes
The space between us widens
And how to swim for you?

And how to swim for you?
To wade across that dry river
Of dreams never slept
Is the problem

A wet moon

A love poem I cannot write
But watch thoughts roll from a cigar smoke
The expression of a silent longing
Time —arrested in a matchbox

Time's toothless impatience,
Like an offending reminder slowly staggers
To hang my mind on the nail of her departure

I hear daily the nights murmured pulses
And pleasure's screams of a teenage girl,
Willingly I have measured memories of her
Rewound them as the moon across the sky
Drowned in the teardrops in my eye

A love poem I cannot write
But wrestle the night to keep its mouth shut
And wait for a knock on the door.

I heard him come

Whose feet I think I hear on the gravel road
Pacing along in this night's insomnia, glad
And slower
Silent, but with a determined effort
Even slower
Yet sure to defy me one more look at her
Will you and I defy the dusty call!
The horn that blows at the day's fall?

Now press ears against the nights' wall
Slow though the hooves on the road
And him whose feet I hear
Is coming….coming…coming…

Which way, I do not know into the dark forest
I fear it
Surely, the depth of the sea is no certainty

The horn blows, the drumbeat will not cease
To tear my soul through the teeth of a smoky night
Notorious hell,
Frightening…
Insistent feet in the night
Dung burns like incense-
Making a sacrifice

Here I cling
To the last leaf on night's gnarled bough
Here they are
The feet

I know to another season
Irredeemable season

You and I will be worlds apart
Neither are the living heroes
Nor the dead defeated!

Love

The heart is a small place
Such a vulnerable place too
To hide, to store these feelings
Of delicate love grenades

And how I fear what it will be
When we two must meet
In the crevice and minefield of love
Where none stays without risks
Nor must escape without scars

Time

Time like a god
Knows all the contents
In its infinite patience
We loiter on its highways
Our purpose engraved in the wrinkles
On our faces

In us the aroused anger of wasps
The consuming anarchy

Of the veld fire
Obliterating every trash
Sparing nothing in its wake

We speak less of love
But more of animosity
With these burning tongues
Drill bits for granitic thoughts

A Letter to my sweetheart

Dear love
Sail with me to the end
Of a troubled earth,
There
True to our promises we made
We will spend long hours
Picking love like it were fruits
Strolling along beaches of memories
Throwing pebbles tenderly, holding
The beams of a trembling sunlight
Summoning like a conspiracy
The insidious longing

A promise

How shall we two meet
In embraces
When eyes will weep
How shall we bring our hands to greet
When cruel nights and days pass on their feet
Persuading us with them to time's end

And when the hawk will not sing to me,
When the sun on its last walk
The nights that wait,
 An emptiness that soaks
I know on your side I will never walk
But to my heart, to my soul
Well-kept like it were a museum, the promises
It will not be what it is
If I fail to love you a countless time

Without end

The days are empty
Like words of a foreign language
Happiness stands in shreds
Like flowers after an electric storm
Loneliness huddles
Like pain on the soul
Darkness settles down
Like formless nostalgia on the heart
These desperate lips share dreams
Like cigars puffing deceptive hope
Into a sky groping for a future

A silent travel

At the brink of the forest
I stand
I can hear still
The clatter of hooves
Of horses,
 Whose rider brought me here
The sun,
 Now distant
Falls,
 I do not fear
The coming of darkness
As I stand here

Not a voice stirs,
All is peaceful and still
The road was winding
 And hard I travelled
And I just wish none of you take it
Tired,
 I wish to find a piece of earth to rest

All clocks on my wall

I am a tree
In the wind, broken at the knee
Bleeding dirges like skies of storms
Atoning in signatures of lightning all men's wrong
All men's folly

I am the wind
Broken in song, and blindly
And voicelessly down the gutter
To the drains where like a shutter
My voice erupts into protest

I am this star
Impeded into the dark skin of the sky
Like a scar, watching man mourn
The blight they are born for

I am the sun
Trapped in the hint of haze
With a mammoth task of an adjudicator
To judge
The divide of day and night
Dazzling I go

Time to part

To have known you
To have gathered you in my embracing eyes
And delicate heart
When the sun's arrowheads at dawn
Tenderly
Cling to the skin of the waking morning
Is part of this pain
That runs like a thread
Of thorny barbed wire through my nerves

Now that the chariot's wheels hurry near
That the feet of the mourners

Embraced in red dust arrive
That the drumbeat thuds in dull throbs
That the wind wallows into a dance of pain
That an owl supplicates
Will you not rush in haste
Tears falling like the Chingoma Falls
To drawn me in the depth of your breasts
Where death and I
Shall spent the night? .

Ecstasy

Brushstrokes on soft sky
First kisses in the rain
Feet pattering and clattering
A wet laughter of tenderness
Passion flings us forth from its sling
The air an ecstasy, our holding frenzied
Reaching lips, hands tough
Electric sparks flare, stars fall
Tears on your face tenderly
Thighs loosen, heart walls up
An engine roars, life erupts like a coiled spring
Jesus enters Jerusalem, an ecstasy
A cry, a belch, a heavy sigh
 Thunder crashes its headaches
Entire row,
I come again and again
Racing to the edge-insanity, falling
Into the sky tumbling
OH!

A prayer from the cemetery

For us,
All passage-ways are in barricades
We decay here in sin for a thousand decades
Waiting for a second coming,
Supplicating
Singing invocations,
Pouring libations
Burning incense…

Descend,
Leap
Leap against fires of our anguish
The fires of blazing darkness
Be swift,
Make haste to bring us rest
Transfix us in thunder, in rain
Purge us and earth
Purge us from this rust
In both eyes we are blind

In our wild screams
We have no voice, no speech
Come,
Lead us by your hand
We know beyond this is a lurid hinterland
There is neither Love nor peace here
But this silenced pain
Reclined with us in the cemeteries

This is no mere recital
We are broken ancient walls

Come salvage us our wreckage
And preserve us in the architecture of eternity
Again and again
To witness
Creation!

Your smile

I like your commodious smile
Razzmatazz sunset and sunrise are both there
Despair and hope suckle the same bitter breasts

Now the tree of longing has grown
The dry leaves scattered on the lawn
A new season buds in my heart.

And behind me
The years collapse
Keeping me going
As a wall watch
Counts with each stroke
The destiny of millions

But until then when I meditate
Debating of death and doubt
Let me a while
Play hockey in the yard of your smile
My love

Angel 1

Since we are mortals
Fate!
Whose destination is this life?
Fate
Whose logical conclusion is this death?
I worry day and night,
Each step to stumble

And where to find you
In the desert and dust
How to embrace you
In the arms before sunset?

At the back of my mind
I have each of the million possibilities
Opening the doors
To find only you
Arrested in the vastness of your absence

While the hills are young
Make a bed of roses in the sun!

Angel 2

Angel, my angel
You are the sweet dream
Which over and over again
I long to sleep

Today
Before six o'clock
Before the sun hides away beyond the rocks
Angel,
Plait a sweet song for me
Sing of the roses flowering on the moon
Sing of the green grass on the clouds
Sing of the love
In the crevice and dungeons of your heart
Come!
Let us go,
Give me your hand
Let us go you and me
There,
We will be forgetful of how life may end
There,
In each other's arms we will lie
There,
In each other's face we will cry
There,
I will sleep between your breasts
Waiting more purposefully for God

Angel
Between us a river flows
Will you not in haste swim across it

I will gather you up in my arms
And love you until the hills grow old

Angel 3

In me Angel
When the night flowers in the moon
When my soul seek yours
Leaping flames of longing ravage

I want
When each day the tears fall
When loneliness stitches the heart
To be hypnotized by the moon in your face

So I desire
When in our separateness we ignite
When the hope to meet glows with dawn
To rest in the embrace of your smile

Angel 4

Take me to Honde Valley
Where late the sun comes
And the mountains stagger into the sky
I want to feel the cold nights
Wrapping their numb hands on me
Tenderly as I search into your soul

I want to see the fog
Descend from the depth of eternity

Softly drowning with us into innocence

I want to hear the water
Whose voice the choir of angles
Wash away the night of human aridity

Emotions flare on a matchstick

Various in their million gazes
The stars of the sky the eye invite
The pulse of my heart only quickens
For that single twinkle
The trickle of tears on your face

Deep in the ransacked mind
Longing's brute staggers home, muttering
So where in this fog to find you
To feel once more that hot breath
When emotions flare on a matchstick?

The happiness of us (Salut de I home)

Now that you are here,
Let us watch the world pass-
Stumbling by, full of cares
Let us into this heaven escape,
Be lost in the petals of longing,
Blooming with each day passing by

There,
Surely, you and I will understand,

The longing on our tongues
Burdened with love,
So,
Let us be together in time without end.

Make a call

When your heart boils
Like a souring wound
And bleeds for a smile
Pick the phone and call

When your days smoke up
And hiccup for breath
Like a chimney puffed up
Pick the phone and call

When your soul burns
Like a heaped pyre
And struggles for life
Pick the phone and call

When your mind is bankrupt
Like the confusion in the mind
And staggers in circles
Pick the phone and call

When your love dries
Like a soul in turmoil
And yearns for only me
Pick the phone and call

Indeed my dear love
Between us a desert romps
And to cross for you
Pour your tears I will swim.

Will you come at noon?

Will you come by noon
Far and silent now the grasslands
Like diarrhea
Time runs to its end
Mere longing out of my breasts
Night welcomes all those defied rest

With you
There your heart lies
The days that are past, the days lonely
Within me your memory and always
Lullabies that die still-born
Forever
I seem to know you are gone!

Hollow Despair

My mind up the mountain,
Climbers
Seeking, like other climbers
On the trail,
The truth in those clouds;

I have sought love

Pure like mountain water
But none down here
Among this garbage
Have I found!

And the peace
Of innocence
 Ancient like the mbira,
Which my mind
Yearns for,
Is not here
Among this wreckage

So deceptive
Emotions
Like a noose around my neck
Command my lot and me
To that tumult-
The hollows of despair;

Though,
Filled with hope
To touch purity,
Weary I stagger,
Tumbling down the ledge
Into a seething heart!

Heavy Terrible Words

My tongue has words
From which fires a speech so terrible
Firing at the illusory glass between us

These words are heavy and terrible
Mud-clogged by the centuries of abuse
That now you must think yourself a God

These words are heavy
M y heart is torn by their sharp edges
They burn me like hot embers

And for how long to endure
A darksome hour
That drags me deathwards
Is this what love had for women?

This which to only a woman pains
When helplessly my kind perishes
Under the ruthless sword
Of a stubborn tradition

And faithful like the sun
I have stood by you
In the very moments
Of your greatest weakness

League of the Night and Fog

Daily
You and I
With teary eyes watch
Men-turned-monsters against their own terror unleash
One by one
Condemned like rabid dogs
We perish
You after me
Into the Night and Fog

The night's insomnia hovers in the howl of a lone dog
The chill of the this death
The scared scream in the night
The patience of one's turn
The patience for one's death
Chattering prayers through gushing teeth
We go

That we die now
Rounded up as cattle
That hope is shattered by the rifle's rattle
Why not fight with these bare bleeding knuckles
So that the world knows
We perished for freedom.

If tomorrow comes

If tomorrow comes
Let there be no love
For me,
No love
No song

Let me walk alone
The length of despair
And feel to the nerve
The sting of loss

Let there be no dangling bridge
Across that raging flood
For I should drown
In my own tears

Let the sun dip its wings
Into the night of my life
For in this silence
I will wait for death
To carry me away
In serenity

Elegy for Muzee!

Now consumed
In the dreaming of eternal clouds
Far removed, for now and unpredictable time to come
Immune to the malady of this earth corruptible
Your footprints clear on the road before us though
Along in the drilling sun, where we must trudge
Knowing well how sinuous the journey
To our destiny, that glimmers in the mirage
Knowing your barefooted soul will lead us
To that crucible, where truth and justice rock on the
cradle
When there, many will break into dance,
Surely!
Perhaps for grief,
Perhaps for joy!
Knowing the rustle of leaves
Is the eternal testimony of you
 Fallen hero!

Deep thoughts

That is when the moon gleams
And the sun shines
When winds rustle in the comfort of summer
And streams swell

A pen vomits its headache
On the palm of a blank page
I get perplexed
My mind boggled
From the effect of loneliness
As it fires into my soul
Like a bolt of lightning

The night opens its thighs
Wind and nostalgia run their promiscuity
To the last leaf of time

I stare at the ceiling
The dampness engulfs me
My voice wrung in the muted screams
As stars fall like gagged teeth

Violent Storm

Terror twins the brain
Hours crawl along but brutally
No feelings
Only this immense pain
From within the depth of despair
Whispers' harsh abrasive words

Shuttering in a ricochet
And softly into songs eyes with tears
Not even a kiss to still
The cradle in the violent storm

Smoke that scribbles illegibly on the sky
Whispers my name
Thunder roars its head
And tears through the eaves
I do not know what is happening
Other violent souls
Crawl in the darkness
And do I have to face the exit
That is entrance to pain
To scream silence out of my yesterdays
To strangle and mangle the voices in me
Hurling words like petrol bombs

Dare I swim for you
A wrecked dream
Dare I ask-
What purpose life can be?
And which one of you dare answer back?

Searching Soul

The dust
Of human impulses
Settles down
This heart
Beats a haste retreat
From the petals of the rising sun
And will not succumb
To the bloodless massacres
Of the soul

The Power of a Woman

Are not women
Such people powerful and
Such diamond pebbles, stubborn hope
Would you were to abandon them and
Cast misery on them and
By all known patriarchal vices make
This hard for them and
 Clamp their mouths and
Stuff their throats with barbed wire and
Put their voices on a shredding machine and
 By the tool of sex dishearten them and
Behind office doors murder them with lust?

You would realize soon
Your life is such a blind moon.

Letters to My Love

The tenderness our longing hearts have
Like wild flowers in bloom
Outgrows this chasm of separation between us
And here I alone feed
On those memories of kisses we made
When we first met in summer
That summer!

For out of this cruel depth of distance
Yearns the groping embrace
Of memories of you well-kept
But, my love, despite this rift
That will keep us further apart by tomorrow
My soul reaches out into space
For your comforting breast's assurance
Yet, despite how the soul is taxed
How the heart suffers
My love, always remember
My longing for you outpaces this suffering-
The pain this world can inflict
On a body of flesh!

Defeat is a Joyful Journey

If I were frail and old
These impulses so slow,
I would not blindly leap
At the fire on these lips

If I were blind
My day to me so kind
I would not see the sky
And those who make me cry

If I were deaf
To deceptive whispers safe
I would not hear
The truth I fear

If I were unborn
To this world unknown
I would not feel this pain
When love brings no gain

If I were strong
Distant to the noose of emotion
I would walk away into the night
Away from anyone's sight

If I were wise, so wise
To read the minds, not to guess
I would not froth on the mouth
In search for the truth

In this crazy city of grey rain

In this crazy city of grey rain
The buildings dream crazy in the sky
Of crazy shortages and crazy prices
The dwellers who crazily hurry across streets
Their destinies a million uncertainties
The cars crazy cockroaches crawling on canes
As they creep and screech on our nerves

The shop shelves whose emptiness greet
And escort us to the shadow of desperation
Where the cloudburst of rising dust
Picks up souls from putrid heaps
Of human hope scattered like landforms
Our million impatient souls whose sanity
Gnarled on the potholed roads of this city
Where neither slogans nor mouthwash platitudes
Can salvage from this wreckage

Grandma

Grandma,
Though old now
Like old dry leaves
Her ancient voice rustles
A resonant whisper of wisdom

From deep the receding life
Whose waves once effaced the shores
Of my thirsty mind
I gather mementoes' ripe fruit

In her dull eyes
Deeper,
Darker than the waiting night
Periodic specks of light
Ignite me out of blindness

Patiently she waits
Though
For reunification with eternity
While a world in her to a tumult races
Once more to witness creation

Nostalgia

You have fears too
That before long the world might collapse
Into the thunderclap of a nuclear war
That candles might eat themselves into flames?

You have these fears too
That the man-inflicted wounds of earth
May not heal
The Satanism that may out-pace piety
And our innocence may lose will
The endless seasons of a disease determined
Our young who may sprout into graveyards?

You have fears too
That shadows may grow and leap like flames
The third world that may rot in poverty
The Jesus who may never turn up again
To salvage us from Noah's wreckage
From the errors of our bare hands?

To the Old People's Home

Will you take me now
To the old people's home
There where they will say:
"How younger he looks!"

And gladly I will join them at tea
With dry bread in cracked wet plates
We will sing new songs from our past

Waiting more purposefully for the sunset
We will page through the dust
Stroll down and up the vistas of time
Counting and recounting the million times
We must have stumbled along the way
Just to meet at this nice home of neglect

Wondering how we have had our children
Grow faster than cabbages
Those who today would have us locked here
Till eternity decides each of our fate

Anyway, take me now
To the old people's home son!

Dry Spell

Though the days
Drag us forth on empty hopes
The labors of our hands
To such vain yielding
Though the seasons stride on
Traversing angular peaks of disillusionment
As the youth mill about closed factories
Singing fear
With gritting teeth out of the future
Though the sky refuses rain
Spell with surplus smoke a dry stroke of thunder
Igniting disease's dynamite sticks
While the shovel continues to plant us
As if drilling this stone provide answers

Though dry our voices
With the mourning, the crying
We must, we must endure!

Home Longing

I think of home
A country
 Far away south
And the red sunsets
The songs of forgotten heroes

I think of childhood,
And the wet tea cups-
The silent tears behind the ears

I think of love
The unfinished, unsent letters-
The mouthfuls of fake kisses

I think of loss
The desperate tears
The wild screams in the night

I think of promises
The chewed ends of lies
The invisible river between us

I think of you my love
And the moon-lit landscapes
The eavesdropping loneliness

True love

If I wronged you, forgive my love
For the errors of earth do set us apart
It will not do at all to do without love
For love is nourishment to the heart

To pause before a kiss is more worthwhile
Than to nurse a broken promise
My love worthwhile too it is to smile a while
Than to mourn for one strung by a noose

For much in life stand in our way
All the same love should tether us together
And like the sun, lights us our way when we stray
Into dark terrains and even further

Elegy for a Dictator!

The day is over!
The dark sun
Homewards descends
The bells toll
And lonely dogs wail
So does the crying wind
Purring through the plains

The dark that comes
Crushing on you
The million impatient stars
 That mock you
And even dearth

That denies you peace
Then
Where shall you go
The past that glares
With blood-shot eyes
The present
The mouth of a guillotine
The future
a scrap yard of dreams dead?

Street Vending

The streets burn,
Chaos shakes conscience's rusty metal
Your indignation devours the vendor's merchandise
As crazy municipal police beat their bare backs

Fear rules here
As each year the guillotine decides
As political abortions make elections stillborn

Cold and smoky with whispers the nights
Tongues leap like whips, lies to ignite
I see you through this fog, I see you
Holding an adze charging like a maddened bull

Your archer tightens
Deadly for an aim, decidedly to silence me
Why I run,
Why I cry
Each day
Each great year

To install you on that throne of fear

To what end then if I ask,
To what end
Upon us and the generations before us
Has sacrifice and honor brought
Except that hill pelting tears hardened?

Letter to Lorraine

I read the stars, as nights pass
Not for love of arithmetic or astrology
Far, far from it Lorraine, far
Neither from some belated religious impulse
But from that sheer brutal agony
The foreboding feeling of missing you
Sometime together when we miss the point
 As you serve dinner to me, and porridge to Joy
We feel time will preserve us for eternity
We lose track of what time has claimed
That I am ageing, and you growing into a mother
Forgetting that even old men have impulses
And exploding hearts seeking fulfillment
Now full of motherly care and zeal
I lose
The touch,
Your tenderness
To these children
Tragic indeed that mother fed me not mine
The dish of love prepared for my father
Now these too sup from the dish for the gods

At the River

I met her at the river
Nyarushangu bursting to the sea
Young she was,
With teenage eyes,
A pouting face
And unforgiving beauty
All accusatory
But burning in innocence

I am going under now
And do not bother
The years will pile on me into centuries
And the falling leaves